# Winter Trees: A photographic guide to common trees and shrubs

By Dominic Price and Leif Bersweden

All proceeds received by the authors will go to
The Species Recovery Trust

Text © Field Studies Council
Photographs © Dominic Price, Leif Bersweden and Ash Mills
ISBN: 978 1 908819 11 6
OP159.

## Preface

Winter trees bridge the gap between the mellow fruitfulness of autumn and the re-birth of nature in the spring. They are reminiscent of bleak landscapes, windblown and lying in dormancy to such a degree that that they can appear dead.

Yet closer inspection reveals a different story; a multitude of slowly swelling buds, often visible in August before the tree has even thought about losing it leaves. These represent thousands of tiny bundles of life, waiting to spring forth with leaf upon leaf, giving a glimpse of hope in the depth of winter.

A quick glance at the bud summary photos on pages 3-9 of this guide instantly reveals their sheer diversity. On the whole they are extremely varied, unique, and often very easy to learn and remember. Add on top of this the difference between types of bark, size of tree and habitat, and it starts to become a much easier art-form than it seems at first.

Whether you are simply out for a winter stroll or carrying out a technical out of season hedgerow survey, this guide will be your perfect companion.

## Acknowledgements

Cover photo by Ash Mills – www.ashmills.com

# Contents

| | | | | |
|---|---|---|---|---|
| Preface | ii | Elder | 25 |
| Acknowledgements | ii | Elm | 26 |
| Introduction | 1 | Field maple | 27 |
| Glossary | 1 | Goat willow | 28 |
| Bud summaries | 3 | Grey poplar | 29 |
| Buds opposite on stem | 4 | Grey willow | 30 |
| Buds alternate / spiralling on stem | 6 | Guelder-rose | 31 |
| Confusable species | 10 | Hawthorn | 32 |
| Species accounts | | Hazel | 33 |
| Alder | 12 | Hornbeam | 34 |
| Alder buckthorn | 13 | Horse chestnut | 35 |
| Apple | 14 | Lime | 36 |
| Ash | 15 | Oak | 37 |
| Aspen | 16 | Rowan | 38 |
| Beech | 17 | Spindle | 39 |
| Birch | 18 | Sweet chestnut | 40 |
| Black poplar | 19 | Sycamore | 41 |
| Blackthorn | 20 | Wayfaring-tree | 42 |
| Buckthorn | 21 | White poplar | 43 |
| Cherry | 22 | White willow | 44 |
| Crack willow | 23 | Whitebeam | 45 |
| Dogwood | 24 | Wild privet | 46 |
| | | Wild service tree | 47 |
| | | Index | 48 |

# Introduction

This guide covers the broad-leaved deciduous species you are most likely to find in the UK and includes a few rarer examples too. In some cases a number of species have been encompassed under one heading and the commonest members of the group have been highlighted in order to make the information concise and accessible to beginners and experts alike.

When identifying trees in the winter, there are four characteristics to look at: **general shape of tree / shrub**, **bark**, **twig structure** and **buds**. All of these are detailed in the species accounts, with accompanying photographs. As a shortcut all the bud photos and descriptions are laid out in the 'Bud summaries' section (p. 3-9), which is divided into opposite and alternate structures. It should be noted that for ease we have grouped all non-opposite structures in the alternate section (some species like oak have more of a spiral layout, but are certainly not opposite).

While most species are fairly easy to separate there are a few that routinely cause problems and these are presented in the 'Confusable species section' where similar species are presented side by side in an easy-to-compare layout. Technical terms have been kept to a minimum throughout the guide but there is a glossary below highlighting some key terms.

# Glossary

**Alternate** – refers to the arrangement of buds on the twig; individual buds are spaced along the twig at regular intervals, alternating either side. **Ⓐ**

**Bud scales** – leafy plates forming a protective covering on a bud. **Ⓑ**

**Catkins** – the flowers of trees such as alder, birch and hazel. **Ⓒ**

**Coppicing** – the act of periodically cutting trees / shrubs down to ground level to encourage the growth of new shoots.

**'Crocodile back'** – refers to the gnarled appearance of the twig in trees such as elm and field maple. **Ⓓ**

**Epicormic growth** – the growth of shoots straight out of the trunk, often accompanied by bulges in the trunk. **E**

**Lateral buds** – buds growing on the sides of the twig. **F**

**Leaf scar** – the mark left on a twig when the leaf falls, it is present just below the bud. **G**

**Lenticels** – corky spots or lines on the stem of a twig that allow the tree to take in air. **H**

**Opposite** – refers to the arrangement of buds on the twig; the buds face each other on opposite sides of the twig, forming individual pairs. **I**

**Pollarding** – the upper branches are periodically cut back to the trunk or to a framework of branches, encouraging dense new growth. Typically a pollarded tree has a short upright trunk with a dense top of branches.

**Spines** – rigid structures arising from the twig that taper to a sharp point. **J**

**Spiralling** – refers to the arrangement of buds on the twig; individual buds are spaced along the twig at regular intervals, alternating either side and spiralling along the twig. **K**

**Suckering** – the growth of new shoots from the base of the tree.

**Terminal bud** – the bud growing at the very end of the twig. **L**

Winter Trees: A photographic guide to common trees and shrubs

## Bud summaries

### Buds **opposite** on the stem (buds may be slightly offset)

Go to **page 4**

### Buds **alternate** on the stem or **spiralling** around the stem

Go to **page 6**

## Buds **opposite** on the stem — In these species the buds face each other

In some species, such as ash and spindle, the buds are occasionally offset from each other but still share the overall characteristics of this group.

**Alder buckthorn** – Page 13
Buds velvety hairy and light brown (can be offset). Bark with vertical orange slits.

**Ash** – Page 15
Buds black and velvety, on grey stems (can be offset). Bark smooth, becoming fissured.

**Elder** – Page 25
Buds comprise miniature shrivelled leaves on warty, pithy stem. Shrub has weak branches.

**Field maple** – Page 27
Buds reddish-brown with white hairy scale edges, often on side twigs. Bark with vertical ridges.

**Spindle** – Page 39
Green opposite / offset buds lying flat on green angled stem. Many-branched shrub.

**Sycamore** – Page 41
Green buds on grey-brown stems. Bark grey and smooth; flaky on older trees.

Winter Trees: A photographic guide to common trees and shrubs

## osite sides of the stem

**Buckthorn** – Page 21
Buds talon-like and often in offset pairs. Twigs pale and generally straight.

**Dogwood** – Page 24
Buds lying close to red (at times green) stem. Red, many-twigged shrub.

**Guelder-rose** – Page 31
Shiny, red-green buds on grey angled stem. Shrub with smooth bark, becoming rougher.

**Horse chestnut** – Page 35
Large, sticky, brown buds. Edges of bark lifting off in older trees.

**Wayfaring-tree** – Page 42
Buds resemble velvety 'fawn ears' on a mealy brown stem. Shrub, bark fissures when old.

**Wild privet** – Page 46
Buds brown-green, dumpy and in opposite / offset pairs. Many-branched shrub; leaves persist during the winter.

## Buds alternate / spiralling on stem   These buds show a variety

**Alder** – Page 12
Reddish purple 'boxing glove' buds on warty ochre twig with catkins and 'cones'.

**Alder buckthorn** – Page 13
Buds are tufted and lack scales; spreading spindly branches. Vertical orange slits in bark.

**Beech** – Page 17
Buds very pointy and on a slender twig. Trunk grey with horizontal wrinkles.

**Birch** – Page 18
Small, green-brown buds on slender twig. Bark peeling, branches drooping.

**Buckthorn** – Page 21
Buds reddish-brown and talon-like. Twigs pale and generally straight.

**Cherry** – Page 22
Red-brown buds, rounded with a point. Horizontal lines on bark.

**Goat willow** – Page 28
Plump yellow-red buds. Bark with vertical gashes and fissures when old.

**Grey poplar** – Page 29
Egg-shaped buds with small white hairs. Bark has diamond-shaped pores.

...arrangements, from alternate to spiralling, but are rarely opposite

**Apple** – Page 14
Reddish-brown, downy-tipped buds, usually stalked. Bark fissures into small, rectangular plates.

**Aspen** – Page 16
Buds dark brown and sharp. Terminal bud has rounded bud scales. Bark fissured.

**Black poplar** – Page 19
Buds brown and sharp. Terminal bud has pointed bud scales. Bark heavily fissured.

**Blackthorn** – Page 20
Very spiny; buds are on twigs and spines. Bark very dark and peeling with age.

**Crack willow** – Page 23
Olive brown buds lying flat against the stem. Twigs brittle, particularly at base.

**Elm** – Page 26
Tiny black buds (c.2 mm). Older trees with 'crocodile back'.

**Grey willow** – Page 30
Small red buds on a slender, downy twig. Bark with diamond-shaped pores.

**Hawthorn** – Page 32
Spiny, buds at base of spines, usually not on them. Bark pale brown and flaking with age.

**Continued over**

## Buds alternate / spiralling on stem — Continued

**Hazel** – Page 33
Plump green through to reddish-brown buds on hairy stem. Smooth grey / brown bark. Often coppiced.

**Hornbeam** – Page 34
Pointy buds on slender twig. Trunk smooth and grey, rather furrowed.

**Rowan** – Page 38
Conical buds on a shiny twig. Smooth grey bark with horizontal scars.

**Sweet chestnut** – Page 40
Plump buds sitting on individual shelves. Bark becoming fissured, then twisting.

**Whitebeam** – Page 45
Green buds with brown margins and white hairs on edges of scales. Bark glossy.

**Wild service-tree** – Page 47
Green, pea-like buds with brown scale edges. Small tree, bark finely fissured with age.

**Lime** – Page 36
Plump buds on red twig (can be green). Suckering freely, very fissured when old.

**Oak** – Page 37
Fat, orange-brown buds with many scales, in terminal clusters; many-branched twigs.

**White poplar** – Page 43
Buds small and thickly downy on a densely felted twig. Bark with diamond-shaped pores.

**White willow** – Page 44
Small brown / yellow buds lying flat against the stem. Slender twig, silky-hairy when young.

# Confusable species

These pages cover some of the more difficult pairs of trees to distinguish between, giving the key differences to aid identification.

**Beech and hornbeam**
- Beech has longer, pointier buds
- Hornbeam twigs are thinner / more delicate
- Beech buds tend to point away from the stem whereas hornbeam buds lie closer to the stem
- Beech twigs are always smooth while hornbeam twigs can be hairy
- Beech bark develops cross-ridges when old; hornbeam bark develops angled furrows.

**Beech** p. 17

**Hornbeam** p. 34

**Common lime and small-leaved lime**
- Common lime twigs tend to be unbranched; small-leaved lime twigs are more divided.

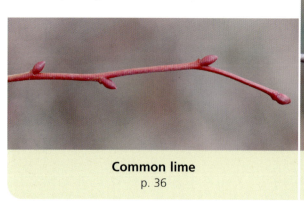

**Common lime** p. 36

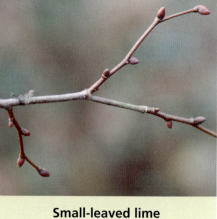

**Small-leaved lime** p. 36

## Confusable species                                        Continued

**Blackthorn and hawthorn**
- Blackthorn has buds on long spines; hawthorn has short spines which rarely bear buds, but will often have a bud growing at the base
- Blackthorn bark peels whereas hawthorn bark tends to flake
- If berries are present (early winter) – blackthorn has black berries, hawthorn has red berries.

**Blackthorn**
p. 20

**Hawthorn**
p. 32

**Silver birch and downy birch**
- Downy birch has hairy twigs that lack warts whereas silver birch has hairless warty twigs
- Downy birch is a more erect tree than silver birch without many drooping branches
- Downy birch twigs are duller and darker than silver birch twigs which are usually shiny
- Young downy birch will have brownish bark that barely peels; young silver birch has pale silvery bark that easily peels.

**Silver birch**
p. 18

**Downy birch**
p. 18

# Alder
*Alnus glutinosa*

### Overall characteristics
- Grows up to 30 m tall
- Damp woodland and by lakes and rivers
- Conical crown, young trees Christmas tree-like in outline
- Woody cone-like fruits usually present (which are the fruiting female catkins) **C**
- Typically adorned with a mass of 'decorations' in the form of the fruits of both male and female catkins
- Visible root nodules when growing in water

### Twigs **D**
- Ochre (young twigs can be greenish)
- Ridged when young
- Orange warts present (these are called lenticels; they allow the tree to exchange gases with its environment)

### Buds **B**
- Reddish-purple, usually bearing a couple of very thin orange lines that run longitudinally (these are glands)
- On short stalks (approximately 3 mm long)
- 'Boxing glove' shaped
- Sometimes have a sticky layer of resin

### Bark **A**
- Purplish brown and smooth when young, soon dark grey-brown
- Fissures over time, eventually cracking into vertical plates
- When cut, the wood becomes a blood-orange colour

# Alder buckthorn
*Frangula alnus*

### Overall characteristics
- Shrub or tree of damp acidic soils (bogs and open damp woodlands)
- Up to 5 m tall
- Spreading spindly branches
- Relatively uncommon

### Twigs C D
- Pale grey to reddish-brown
- Many side stalks bearing terminal buds
- Slightly hairy
- Round, with lots of small, knobbly projections (where you would expect to find buds) that make the twig feel bumpy when you run your finger up it

### Buds B E
- Flap-like, tufted
- Velvety hairy
- No scales

### Bark A
- Slightly rough, with vertical orange slits
- Inner bark is lime green and emits a strong smell

# Apple
*Malus* spp.

### Overall characteristics
- A small tree, growing up to 10 m tall
- Usually found in hedgerows or in woodland
- Check for small apples on the ground (not always present) **D**
- Wilding apples are commoner than crab apples
- It is worth noting that many apparently wild crab apples are in fact naturalised apples derived from discarded apple cores

### Twigs **B E F**
- Greyish-brown, often bearing lichens
- Hairless
- Sometimes thorny **F**
- Short twigs grow out of the trunk and branches at regular intervals, giving the tree an untidy look

### Buds **C**
- Reddish-brown
- Oval-shaped with downy tips
- Alternate
- Usually stalked

### Bark
- Deep brown
- Fissures into small, irregular, rectangular plates
- Often covered in mosses and lichen

# Ash
*Fraxinus excelsior*

### Overall characteristics ⓐ
- Slim, tall (up to 30 m)
- Domed top
- Widely-spaced branches
- Some bear clumps of winged seeds in early autumn ⓔ
- Locally abundant, tending to grow on damper soils

### Twigs ⓓ
- Grey (but can be greenish)
- Stem flattened below the buds
- Tend to be very straight
- Lack a ridge between the buds

### Buds ⓒⓓ
- Velvet matt black
- Opposite pairs (can be offset)
- Larger terminal buds

### Bark ⓑ
- Pale grey
- Smooth when young, becomes heavily lined with age as a pattern of vertical fissures develops

# Aspen
*Populus tremula*

**Overall characteristics**
- Upright, slender, to 20 m
- Narrow crown
- Grows in a range of habitats, generally on damper soil
- Similar species see black poplar (p. 19)

**Twigs** C
- Brown, becoming grey
- Hairless (sometimes slightly hairy at tip)
- Smooth

**Buds** B C D
- Dark brown bud scales
- Lying flat against the stem
- Sharply pointed, sometimes curving back towards the twig
- Terminal bud has round-tipped bud scales
- Buds towards the end of the twig may have short white hairs

**Bark** A
- Pale grey / cream with horizontal rows of diamond-shaped pores
- Develops brown fissures with age

# Beech
*Fagus sylvatica*

### Overall characteristics
- Grows up to 40 m tall
- Young trees are slim and conical
- Old trees can get very big and are many-branched and domed
- Young trees and hedges retain dead, copper-coloured leaves in winter
- Similar species see hornbeam (p. 10 and 34)

### Twigs D
- Thin, reddish-brown
- Young twigs may have a few long hairs
- Small, pale spots present, usually in abundance (called lenticels)
- Often zigzagging

### Buds C
- Long and slender (1-2 cm long), spreading from twig
- Tapering to a relatively sharp point
- Scales are large and copper-coloured, eventually developing a whitish tip

### Bark A B
- Smooth and grey
- Older trees first develop horizontal wrinkles and then criss-crossing ridges and furrows

# Birch
*Betula* spp.

### Overall characteristics
- Grows up to 30 m tall
- Distinctive drooping branches in silver birch
- Downy birch more erect than silver birch
- Very straight trunk
- Usually grows in woods, heaths and on the edge of bogs

### Twigs
- Slender, dark brown with a purple tint
- Often with catkins
- If hairy it will be downy birch, hairless and warty silver birch (however hybrids are common, so this isn't definitive). Also see p. 11

### Buds
- Small and shiny
- Pointed
- Hints of pale green and orangey brown

### Bark
- Becoming deeply fissured and knobbly on older trees
- Peeling and papery (far more so in silver birch)
- Young trees with silvery grey bark will most likely be silver birch
- Young trees with brownish bark will most likely be downy birch (this is not definitive)
- Silver birch has dark diamond shaped patches (lenticels)

# Black poplar
*Populus nigra* ssp. *betulifolia*

### Overall characteristics
- Large tree growing to 35 m
- Mature trees with a vast, spreading crown
- Branches arch downwards
- Don't mistake for hybrid black poplar which has ascending branches and a more open canopy
- A rare species; protected from uprooting under the Wildlife & Countryside Act (1981)
- Similar species see aspen (p. 16)

### Twigs
- Slender at first, becoming chunky and knobbly
- Medium to golden brown
- Appearing hairless, almost glossy, but usually with fine hairs, particularly at the base of the buds

### Buds
- Medium to dark brown, hairless and shiny
- Sharply pointed
- Generally at least 7 mm long, lying flat against the stem
- Terminal bud has pointed bud scales

### Bark
- Grey
- Very fissured
- Large knobbly bosses

# Blackthorn
*Prunus spinosa*

### Overall characteristics
- Shrub, usually in hedgerows or scrub but occasionally as free-standing tree to 4 m
- Spines almost always present **B**
- Early spring, flowers before it produces leaves
- Many-branched and freely suckering, forming thickets
- Black berries (sloes) persist into the winter **E**
- Similar species see hawthorn (p. 11 and 32)

### Twigs **B**
- Bear several long spines which may eventually bear leaves and flowers / fruit themselves. Some can be large (exceeding 7 cm in length, appearing to be separate side-shoots)
- Dark coloured, some young twigs develop a silvery outer layer
- Young twigs slightly hairy
- Branched in many directions (usually sticking out at 45-90° from the stem)

### Buds **C D**
- Grow on the spines as well as on the stem
- Occasionally in clusters **C**

### Bark **A**
- Black / brown and rough, often powdered with algae
- On older specimens starts to peel

# Buckthorn
*Rhamnus cathartica*

**Overall characteristics**
- Spreading deciduous tree to 6 m
- Often found growing as a shrub in a hedgerow
- Young twigs sprouting from the trunk
- Spines sometimes present

**Twigs D**
- Very straight, particularly the younger twigs
- Greyish-brown; young twigs are pale grey
- Some bearing thin spines
- When broken they have a strong odour
- Lenticels, when present, are sparse

**Buds B C E**
- Reddish-brown, talon-like
- In heavily staggered or perfect opposite pairs; sometimes spiralling along the twig
- Pressed closely against the stem
- Older branches have single buds borne upon stalks B

**Bark A**
- Orange patches can been seen between fissures
- Becoming dark brown with age and beginning to flake
- Lichens and mosses obscure colour

A

B

C

E

D

# Cherry
*Prunus* spp.

### Overall characteristics
- Native deciduous tree, often planted
- Wild cherry up to 30 m, bird cherry tends to be a much smaller tree or a large shrub
- High, domed crown
- Often retaining dead leaves strung out as if on a washing line

### Twigs
- Relatively straight, often curving up at the ends
- Peeling pale grey layer, red-brown underneath
- Smooth

### Buds
- Red-brown, rounded with a point
- Visible scales
- Often at end of multiple scars – like a 'pile of pancakes'
- Single in bird cherry, in clusters of up to 9 in wild cherry

### Bark
- Characteristic orangey brown horizontal lines (lenticels)
- Grey to red
- Shiny in bird cherry, matt in wild cherry
- Peels when young, rough when old

# Crack willow
*Salix fragilis*

### Overall characteristics
- Grows to 25 m as a tree but will often be pollarded
- Broad, spreading crown
- Pendulous branches
- Prefers wet places; it is usually found growing on the banks of rivers and streams
- Similar species see p. 44; be aware of hybrids

### Twigs
- Olive brown
- Spindly
- Brittle where they join with the branch (when bent back at the base a distinct 'crack' can be heard)
- Usually hairless but sometimes slightly downy

### Buds
- Olive brown, the same colour as the twig
- Flattened against the twig
- Bud tip often curves away from the stem, resembling a duck's beak
- Spiralling
- Typically 5-7 mm long

### Bark
- Initially begins to crack into plates
- Becomes rugged and fissured

# Dogwood
*Cornus sanguinea*

### Overall characteristics
- Shrub, growing to 4 m tall
- Tends to occupy scrub or hedgerows
- Easily identifiable from a distance due to its red twigs
- Prefers calcareous soils
- Suckering
- Other varieties are sometimes used as ornamental plantings

### Twigs
- Blood red (can be green in the shade)
- Smooth
- Pale spots usually present (lenticels)

### Buds
- Dark brown, in opposite pairs
- Lying flat alongside stem
- Slightly hairy
- No scales

### Bark
- The more mature specimens have ridged bark
- When bruised it gives off a putrid smell

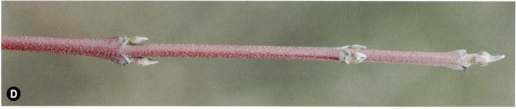

# Elder
*Sambucus nigra*

### Overall characteristics
- A bushy shrub (to 10 m) with many stems arising at ground level
- The pith inside the stalks resembles white, spongy cork
- Grows in a variety of habitats, including scrub, hedgerows, waste ground and woods
- Very common around rabbit warrens as rabbits don't eat elder

### Twigs C
- Often brittle, hollow / contain white pith
- Angled surface giving a fluted appearance
- Prominent warts (these are lenticels)
- Unpleasant smell when crushed (likened to cat urine)

### Buds D
- In opposite pairs
- Very untidy
- No scales; the apparent 'buds' are in fact young leaves, although brown and shrivelled

### Bark B
- Pale brown, corky
- Deeply grooved, particularly when mature
- Frequently covered in mosses and liverworts

# Elm
*Ulmus* spp. (*U. procera* and *U. glabra*)

### Overall characteristics B
- Tall (growing to 35 m)
- Relatively narrow oblong-shaped tree
- Usually grows in hedgerows; full size trees are uncommon due to Dutch elm disease
- English elm freely suckers
- Elms are a complex group of trees and often difficult to distinguish between

### Twigs B C D
- Hairy at first, becoming smooth
- Often have corky 'crocodile backs', some thinner twigs developing 'corky-wings'
- Vertical branches resemble TV aerials B

### Buds D E
- Black (or dark brown)
- Tiny (c. 2 mm)
- Often have very tiny rust-coloured hairs, particularly in wych elm

### Bark A
- Smooth at first, becoming fissured

# Field maple
*Acer campestre*

### Overall characteristics
- Can reach 20 m in height as a tree, although often grows as a shrub
- Very round in profile (although old trees can reach a considerable height and girth)
- The ends of the branches tend to droop before turning upwards
- Often found in hedgerows and woodlands

### Twigs C D
- Light brown and slightly hairy
- Many developing characteristic 'stripes'
- Older twigs have 'crocodile back'

### Buds F G
- Reddish-brown with visible white hairy edges
- Opposite pairs, often on stalks E

### Bark
- Grey or dark brown
- Fine, shallow, vertical fissures that get more evident with age
- Older specimens start losing flakes

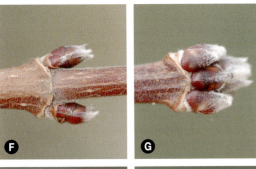

## Goat willow
*Salix caprea*

### Overall characteristics
- Upright shrub or tree, growing to 10 m
- Grows in damp woodland, occasionally in hedgerows and scrub
- Similar species see p. 30; be aware of hybrids

### Twigs D
- Young twigs are lime green, becoming dark brown and budless with age
- Smooth; slightly hairy at first but soon becoming hairless
- Second year twigs lack raised ridges on the wood under the bark

### Buds C E
- Yellow at first, becoming red, particularly towards the end of the twig
- Plump, generally pointing away from the stem
- Hairless
- When broken open cottony inside
- Typically c.5 mm long
- Tend to congregate at the end of the twig
- Terminal and penultimate buds tend to be very close together

### Bark A B
- Pale grey and dotted with diamond-shaped pores
- Fissures develop when old, initially revealing orangey brown wood

# Grey poplar
*Populus* x *canescens*

### Overall characteristics Ⓐ
- A tall tree, potentially reaching 35 m in height
- Usually found in river valleys
- The hybrid between white poplar (p. 43) and aspen (p. 16)

### Twigs ⒸⒹ
- Reddish brown to grey
- Can be very branched
- Slightly hairy

### Buds ⒸⒺ
- Egg-shaped
- Slightly pointed
- The bottom half of each bud scale has whitish hairs
- Bud scales reddish brown
- Often on a short stalk with plentiful leaf scars

### Bark Ⓑ
- Pale grey with horizontal lines of diamond-shaped pores
- Older bark is brown and fissured

# Grey willow
*Salix cinerea*

### Overall characteristics
- Typically a shrub but can grow as a tree to 10 m
- Common in wet woodland and marshes
- Similar species see p. 28 and 44; be aware of hybrids

### Twigs E F
- Reddish brown (can appear greenish with algae)
- Downy, particularly towards the end
- Can be very branched
- Second year twigs, when stripped of their bark, have fine raised longitudinal ridges on the wood C
- In older, thicker twigs these ridges become enlarged and easily visible D

### Buds E F
- Generally red, sometimes yellow-orange when in the shade
- Lying flat against the stem
- Small, typically c.3mm
- Evenly spaced along the twig
- When broken open cottony inside
- Downy

### Bark A B
- Pale grey with horizontal lines of diamond-shaped pores
- Older bark is brown and fissured

# Guelder-rose
*Viburnum opulus*

### Overall characteristics
- Shrub 2-4 m tall
- Typically found on chalk and limestone habitats
- Bright red berries which, when ripe, have an unpleasant odour **B**

### Twigs **C E**
- Grey, angled and hairless
- Twig ends in a withered stalk (where the berries were) **C**
- Pithy inside

### Buds **D E F**
- Younger buds slender, becoming bulbous with age
- Opposite pairs
- Smooth, and shiny
- Reddish-green
- Superficially similar to pomegranate seeds when mature

### Bark **A**
- Pale and smooth in young trees, becoming rougher with age

# Hawthorn
*Crataegus monogyna*

### Overall characteristics **A**
- Shrub (to 15 m) commonly found in hedgerows and scrub, although it is often present in woodland
- Occasionally occurs as a free-standing tree
- Often planted as field boundaries
- Similar species see blackthorn (p. 11 and 20)

### Twigs **D E**
- Small thorns usually present, but not always
- Green to reddish brown when young; otherwise grey
- Often zigzagging

### Buds **C E F**
- Small, oval-shaped
- Slightly reddish
- Can be at the end of multiple scars – 'pile of pancakes' **F**
- Found at base of thorns, seldom on them

### Bark **B**
- Greyish brown
- When older starts flaking off in rough rectangles

# Hazel
*Corylus avellana*

### Overall characteristics
- Most frequently found as coppice: shrubs in managed woodland are up to 4 m but those in unmanaged coppices can outgrow this
- Common hedgerow shrub
- Suckering, producing many stems

### Twigs B D
- Pale brown, softly furry when young (older specimens retain hairs at the shoot tip)
- Slightly zigzagged
- Often with catkins B and / or female buds C (which flower February onwards)

### Buds D E
- Green through to reddish brown
- Large visible scales that have a thin brown edge
- Plump, oval-shaped

### Bark A
- Smooth and shiny, from grey to reddish brown
- Very visible horizontal warts (lenticels)
- Tends to peel

# Hornbeam
*Carpinus betulus*

### Overall characteristics
- Frequently found in parks and ornamental hedges, native to the south of England
- Frequently pollarded
- Rather like a smaller version of beech but branches more outward growing
- Similar species see beech (p. 11 and 17)

### Twigs
- Brown, often zigzagged
- Slightly hairy

### Buds
- Pale brown (can be orangey) with visible elongated scales
- Buds lie close to the stem (whereas in beech they tend to stick out more) and often curve inwards slightly

### Bark
- Grey and smooth when young, but angled (not rounded)
- Older trees develop furrows

# Horse chestnut
*Aesculus hippocastanum*

### Overall characteristics
- Can be huge (to 25 m). Often found in parkland
- Branches arch down and then out
- Usually planted but regularly self-seeds

### Twigs D E
- Greyish brown
- Covered in protruding white spots (lenticels)
- Typically un-branched
- Horseshoe-shaped leaf scars C

### Buds B E
- Very sticky
- Large, with visible scales
- Dark brown
- Can grow on short stalks

### Bark A
- Grey-brown, often covered in powdery lichen and algae
- Becomes flaky in older trees, with edges lifting off tree

# Lime
*Tilia* spp. (*T.* x *europaea* and *T. cordata*)

### Overall characteristics
- Large trees (growing up to 45 m tall)
- Downwards arching branches and twigs
- Hybrids widely planted in parks as well as in woodland
- Common lime often displays epicormic growth (twigs and bulges) on the lower trunk **B**
- Common lime is the hybrid between small-leaved lime and large-leaved lime, rarely found naturally with both parent trees present

### Twigs **D E**
- Very red when young (can be green) and waxy-smooth
- Common lime freely suckers from the base of the tree; small-leaved lime does not do this
- Can be very zigzagged
- Common lime twigs are linear; small-leaved lime twigs tend to be more branched (p. 10)

### Buds **C D**
- Blunt, rounded
- Alternate on stem
- Red-purple (occasionally green)

### Bark **A B**
- Young tree smooth, sometimes lightly cracked
- Old trees become very fissured
- Common lime has large lumps on the lower trunk

# Oak
*Quercus* spp. (*Q. robur* and *Q. petraea*)

### Overall characteristics
- Large robust trees up to 30 m
- Very branched
- Often with epicormic growth (twigs and bulges on trunk) B
- As a rough guide, pedunculate oak is the dominant species in English lowlands, sessile oak is more dominant in upland oak woods
- These species hybridise very commonly so beware of intermediates

### Twigs D
- Grey to brown with pale warts
- Often with a thin silvery peeling layer
- Many-branched

### Buds C E
- Orangey brown, plump
- Many-scaled with waxy hairless scales
- Terminal buds in a cluster
- More than 20 scales probably sessile oak, fewer than 20 probably pedunculate oak
- If you can find acorn cups, pedunculate oak are on stalks (usually 2-3 cm long but can reach 8 cm), sessile oak are unstalked

### Bark B
- Smooth at first
- Vertically fissured from young age

# Rowan
*Sorbus aucuparia*

### Overall characteristics
- Smallish tree, up to 16 m
- Branches tend to grow upwards
- Frequently found in upland areas on acidic soils, less common in lowlands (although often planted in parks or gardens)

### Twigs
- Upwards growing
- Grey or sometimes shiny brown
- Very smooth
- Young twigs usually have some long hairs

### Buds
- Conical
- Often on very short stalks
- Slightly purple scales, hairy scale edges (can be very hairy)
- Far apart on twig

### Bark
- Grey and smooth
- Horizontal scars

# Spindle
*Euonymus europaeus*

### Overall characteristics
- Many-branched shrub or small tree (to 6 m)
- Occurs on calcareous soils
- Spectacular orange / pink fruit persisting into early winter **B**
- 'Spindly' look about it

### Twigs **E G**
- Noticeably green
- Angled stems, with flat faces **C**
- Thicker twigs become rectangular in cross-section
- Prominent side-branches on twigs
- Lack a ridge between the buds

### Buds **D F G**
- Small, opposite (can be offset)
- Pale green with reddish brown scale margins
- Lying flat on stem

### Bark **A**
- Pale brown to grey
- 'Rippling' surface

# Sweet chestnut
*Castanea sativa*

## Overall characteristics
- Common tree in south-east England, often planted elsewhere
- Often coppiced but when mature can grow up to 25 m
- Look for spiny nut cases on ground
- Branches arch down, often touching ground

## Twigs D
- Shiny, smooth with prominent longitudinal ridges
- Sometimes covered in white dusting which comes off when rubbed
- Deep ochre, angled, with warts
- Tend to grow straight
- Small white spots (lenticels)

## Buds C E
- Light brown / red, sometimes with light green sections
- Plump, sat on 'shelves'
- Alternate

## Bark A B
- Smooth brown on young
- Surface fissures longitudinally on older specimens, then starts to spiral

# Sycamore
*Acer pseudoplatanus*

### Overall characteristics
- Spindly sapling through to huge veterans (30 m)
- Wide crown
- Very common, often one of the first trees to colonise unmanaged land

### Twigs ⓒ
- Grey-brown with small spots (lenticels)

### Buds ⓑⓓ
- Pale green opposite pairs
- Large scales with purple edges and a fringe of very small white hairs ⓓ

### Bark ⓐ
- Completely smooth and grey on young trees
- On older trees starts to flake off in rectangular chunks

# Wayfaring-tree
*Viburnum lantana*

### Overall characteristics
- Shrub to 6 m
- Blends in very well with surrounding vegetation
- Typically found on chalk, more common in the south-east of England

### Twigs D
- Deep ochre with mealy white or yellow coating
- Typically very round, but can be angled

### Buds B C
- Resemble velvety fawn ears
- Mustard to grey coloured with mealy coating
- No scales
- Strong opposite pairs, never on stalks
- Can be either lying close to the stem or spreading away from it
- Distinctive terminal flower bud E

### Bark A
- Grey to brown
- Smooth when young, becoming fissured

# White poplar
*Populus alba*

### Overall characteristics
- Grows to 25 m
- Broad, spreading crown
- Commonly found in parkland; planted on roadsides, as windbreaks and occasionally on coastal dunes
- Similar species see grey poplar (p. 29)

### Twigs
- Young twigs covered in a dense white felt
- Soon become hairless and grey
- Curve upwards at the end

### Buds
- Thickly downy buds on young twigs
- Becoming reddish-brown with age
- Bluntly pointed
- Buds on second year twigs are on short stalks that are laden with leaf scars

### Bark
- Smooth and pale grey at first, with diamond-shaped pores
- Over time vertical fissures develop

# White willow
*Salix alba*

### Overall characteristics
- Grows up to 25 m tall
- Very much a waterside species
- Commonly pollarded
- Similar species see p. 23 and 30; be aware of hybrids

### Twigs
- Olive brown when young
- Becoming dark grey with age
- New shoots are silky-hairy but eventually become hairless

### Buds
- Buds lying flat against the stem
- Covered in many off-white hairs, particularly those towards the end of the twig
- Brown / yellow; sometimes reddish
- Oval-shaped, tapering to a blunt point
- Typically 4-5 mm long

### Bark
- Smooth and pale grey at first, developing orangey fissures
- Mature trees are dark grey with deep fissures

# Whitebeam

*Sorbus aria* agg.

### Overall characteristics
- Complex group of micro-species
- Look for large white leaves on ground below

### Twigs
- Robust
- Dull purplish-brown
- Hairless
- Young twigs reddish brown

### Buds
- Green with brown margins
- Fringe of white hairs on scale edge
- Alternate or spiralling
- Oval-shaped, with a blunt point
- Often on short stalks; each stalk has multiple leaf scars

### Bark
- Glossy
- Smooth, with wavy ridges on older specimens

# Wild privet
*Ligustrum vulgare*

### Overall characteristics **A B C**
- Spreading shrub often in hedgerows, but also frequent in the understory of calcareous woodlands
- Very branched
- Semi-evergreen **C**
- Small, black berries can persist into January **B**
- Garden privet is a common escapee

### Twigs **E**
- Straight and very round
- Characteristically growing upwards
- Young twigs downy
- Lack a ridge between the buds
- Brittle
- Typically covered in pale lenticels

### Buds **D E F**
- Egg-shaped, dumpy
- Scales usually dark brown-green with a thin pale margin
- Occasionally green with brown tips
- Opposite pairs; mostly staggered but some perfectly opposite

### Bark
- Reddish-brown
- Vertical gashes present on older shrubs
- Often covered in algae

# Wild service-tree
*Sorbus torminalis*

### Overall characteristics A
- Medium-sized tree (to 20 m)
- Spreading or domed, depending on where it is situated
- Scarce, but occasionally locally common, especially in ancient woodland. It is rare to find many trees growing together

### Twigs C
- Slender, brown and often shiny
- Spreading
- Commonly forking
- Small, pale spots (lenticels)

### Buds C D
- Distinctly green, pea-like
- Rounded, oval-shaped to spherical
- Obvious scales with brown edges
- Alternate
- Commonly borne upon short stalks

### Bark B
- Greyish-brown
- Rough and finely fissured with age

# Index

Main entries are in **bold**

## Latin names

*Acer campestre* **27**
   *pseudoplatanus* **41**
*Aesculus hippocastanum* **35**
*Alnus glutinosa* **12**
*Betula* spp. **18**
*Carpinus betulus* **34**
*Castanea sativa* **40**
*Cornus sanguinea* **24**
*Corylus avellana* **33**
*Crataegus monogyna* **32**
*Euonymus europaeus* **39**
*Fagus sylvatica* **17**
*Frangula alnus* **13**
*Fraxinus excelsior* **15**
*Ligustrum vulgare* **46**
*Malus* spp. **14**
*Populus alba* **43**
   *nigra* ssp. *betulifolia* **19**
   *tremula* **16**
   x *canescens* **29**
*Prunus* spp. **22**
   *spinosa* **20**
*Quercus* spp. **37**
   *petraea* **37**
   *robur* **37**
*Rhamnus cathartica* **21**
*Salix alba* **44**
   *caprea* **28**
   *cinerea* **30**
   *fragilis* **23**
*Sambucus nigra* **25**
*Sorbus aria* **45**
   *aucuparia* **38**
   *torminalis* **47**
*Tilia* spp. **36**
   *cordata* **36**
   x *europaea* **36**

*Ulmus* spp. **26**
   *glabra* **26**
   *procera* **26**
*Viburnum lantana* **42**
   *opulus* **31**

## Common names

Alder 1, 6, **12**
Alder buckthorn 4, 6, **13**
Apple 7, **14**
Ash 4, **15**
Aspen 7, **16**, 19, 29
Beech 6, 10, **17**, 34
Birch 1, 6, 10, **18**
Black poplar 7, 16, **19**
Blackthorn 7, 10, **20**, 32
Buckthorn 5, **21**
Cherry 6, **22**
Crack willow 7, **23**
Dogwood 5, **24**
Elder 4, **25**
Elm 1, 7, **26**
Field maple 1, 4, **27**
Goat willow 6, **28**
Grey poplar 6, **29**, 43
Grey willow 7, **30**
Guelder-rose 5, **31**
Hawthorn 7, 10, 20, **32**
Hazel 1, 8, **33**
Hornbeam 8, 10, 17, **34**
Horse chestnut 5, **35**
Lime 9, 10, **36**
Oak 1, 9, **37**
Rowan 8, **38**
Spindle 4, **39**
Sweet chestnut 8, **40**
Sycamore 4, 5, **41**
Wayfaring-tree 5, **42**
White poplar 9, 29, **43**
White willow 9, 30
Whitebeam 8, **45**
Wild privet 5, **46**
Wild service-tree 8, **47**